Marco Lopes Marques

Evaluation of a mindfulness and positive psychology programme

Marco Lopes Marques

Evaluation of a mindfulness and positive psychology programme

ScienciaScripts

Imprint

Any brand names and product names mentioned in this book are subject to trademark, brand or patent protection and are trademarks or registered trademarks of their respective holders. The use of brand names, product names, common names, trade names, product descriptions etc. even without a particular marking in this work is in no way to be construed to mean that such names may be regarded as unrestricted in respect of trademark and brand protection legislation and could thus be used by anyone.

Cover image: www.ingimage.com

This book is a translation from the original published under ISBN 978-613-8-41818-4.

Publisher:
Sciencia Scripts
is a trademark of
Dodo Books Indian Ocean Ltd. and OmniScriptum S.R.L publishing group

120 High Road, East Finchley, London, N2 9ED, United Kingdom
Str. Armeneasca 28/1, office 1, Chisinau MD-2012, Republic of Moldova, Europe

ISBN: 978-620-6-12779-6

Thank you very much.

My arrival at the end of my university career was the result of countless efforts, lessons, experiences and encounters. I am convinced today that, more than anything else, it was these encounters that guided me step by step towards who I am today and what kind of psychologist I will be. It's a very small tribute that I'm paying to all the people who have supported me along the way, but I'd like to offer them all my thanks.

First and foremost, I'd like to thank my mother, who has never lost a shred of confidence in me over all these years. She was there every time I took a wrong step, every doubt, every fear, to light my way and help me move forward. For all that you are and all that you have enabled me to be, I am deeply grateful.

I'd like to thank Océane Sotéras who was incredibly patient with me. Her gentleness and temperance were invaluable allies at all times. I'd also like to thank my best friend Aurélie Cessat, who knows me better than anyone and whose speeches of support I've lost count of. I'd also like to thank Audrey Fontaine, whose kindness and humanism have touched me at every turn. I would also like to thank Cécile Dantzer, who put up with my countless emails and questions and whose insights were more than welcome. I would also like to thank all the patients I have met who, through their life stories, have enriched my own view of Man and his marvellous complexity.

Then I'd like to thank all the people who have helped me to grow and develop, whether directly or indirectly, throughout my time here, and I couldn't possibly name them all: my family, my friends, my fellow students and my teachers.

Finally, I'd like to thank the authors who have guided my thinking and my most important choices, and whose thoughts are always with me: Marcus Aurelius, Dan Milmann and Christophe André.

TABLE OF CONTENTS:

Summary

Introduction: In recent years, interventions based on mindfulness meditation and positive psychology theories have been the subject of much research in many areas of psychology and health. These two approaches have been evaluated as beneficial for improving quality of life and reducing anxiety, depression and ruminative symptoms (Kabat-Zinn, 1982; Lyubomirsky, 2008). The literature now tells us that chronic illnesses can encourage the emergence of this type of symptomatology (Thombs et al., 2006) and have an impact on patients' quality of life (Erpelding et al., 2009). **Objective**: In this study, we propose to evaluate the effect of these two types of approach on quality of life, anxiety, depression and ruminations in a population of patients with chronic illness. **Method**: A total of 8 participants suffering from chronic illness were divided into two interventions. One based on mindfulness meditation (MBI, N=4) and the other based on positive psychology approaches (CARE for Compassion, Attention, Relation, Commitment, N=4). Using test-retest measures, each participant completed the SF-36, the Hospital Anxiety Depression Scale (HADS) and the Mini-Certs. **Results**: Statistical analysis revealed no significant effect of the two interventions on the variables measured. **Conclusion**: We found a difference in means in some of our results, particularly for the SF-36. However, the lack of significance does not allow us to validate our hypotheses or to conclude on a possible effect of our interventions. We can imagine that on a larger population and with a re-evaluation over a longer period, the analysis could reveal significant effects.

Key words : Positive psychology - Mindfulness - Quality of life - Ruminations - Anxiety - Depression - Chronic illness

Supervisor: Cécile Dantzer

CHAPTER 1

I. Introduction

At a time when our life expectancy has never been so high, chronic illnesses are becoming real thorns in our societies which, as well as impacting on our quality of life, can also alter it. The treatments imposed, the arduous nature of certain diets to be adhered to, the activities sometimes limited by our state of health, the possible dependence on technical and medical resources mean that individuals affected by a chronic organic pathology can find their lives turned upside down.

These different elements inherent in the chronically ill condition may constitute factors conducive to the emergence of emotions, cognitions, behaviours and psychological distress (Moullec, Lavoie & Sultan, 2012). As the literature shows, symptoms of anxiety, depression, stress, despair and even suicidal ideation can accompany the daily lives of people with chronic illnesses, which can have repercussions on the development or maintenance of their quality of life (Elliot, Renier & Palcher, 2003; Sharma, Kedesia, Shi & Gandhi, 2016). Life satisfaction can be particularly affected in chronic illness situations where physical pain is a daily occurrence (Boonstra, Reneman Stewart., Schiphorst Preuper, 2013). In 16 to 45% of cases, minor or major depression may occur in the context of cardiovascular disease (Thombs et al., 2006). A 2004 study also revealed that over 40% of patients with type 2 diabetes reported an inadequate sense of psychological well-being (Skovlund, 2004). A 2011 meta-analysis also reported a twofold increase in the frequency of depression in patients with chronic migraines (Antonaci et al., 2011). We also find affective disturbances in people with chronic low back pain, who experience a high level of stress and anxiety, increasing their hypervigilance to pain (Tang et al., 2009). In addition to these disorders, the literature also tells us about other problems associated with these situations, such as feelings of isolation, exclusion and frustration due to the restriction of family activities (Beaumont et al., 2013). Dietary restriction can also have an impact on quality of life, as has been observed in people with type 2 diabetes (Erpelding et al., 2009).

Health psychology, defined by Matarazzo (1980) as "the synthesis of the educational, scientific and practical contributions of psychology to the promotion and maintenance of health, and to the prevention and treatment of disease and associated dysfunctions", is an approach rich in tools, methods and theories for alleviating the difficulties that may be encountered by people whose health has been or is being impaired to the point of affecting their well-being and happiness. Far from focusing solely on the physical or biological aspects of illness, today's care approaches integrate the social, individual, psychological, emotional and behavioural aspects of a person. It is only by including all these elements that we, as health professionals, can hope to offer the best possible care.

Positive psychology was developed with this in mind. Its mission is to identify and develop individual strengths and resources with a view to achieving a certain level of life satisfaction. Numerous interventions have already been developed to contribute to this mission. Shankland, André and Kotsou's CARE (Compassion, Attention, Relation and Commitment) programme (2015) is one such intervention and, reflecting the aims of positive psychology, proposes to develop individuals' emotional, psychological and behavioural resources.

Similarly, research into mindfulness-based interventions has revealed numerous benefits in terms of anxiety-depressive symptomatology (Kabat-Zinn et al., 1992) and psychological distress (Shapiro, Astin, Bishop, & Cordova, 2005), as well as quality of life (Roth & Robbins, 2004). The favourable results from the use of this type of programme in the healthcare environment suggest that patients with chronic illnesses could obtain day-to-day benefits in the management of their treatment on the one hand, but also in their lives in general (Berghmans, 2011).

CHAPTER 2

II. Theoretical framework

    A. Chronic diseases

A.l. Overview and definition of chronic diseases

According to the French Ministry of Health (2011), "a chronic disease is a long-term, progressive illness that is often associated with disability and the threat of serious complications". In 2007, the National Chronic Diseases Plan defined chronic diseases as "the presence of an organic or psychological cause, dating back several months and having an impact on daily life through a functional limitation of activities and participation in social life, with dependence on a treatment, medical technology or the intervention of professionals, and requiring medical or paramedical care, psychological assistance, education or adaptation".

A disease is considered chronic when the technical and medical resources available do not allow it to be cured. Some diseases, such as cystic fibrosis (life expectancy of 40 years today according to the French National Institute for Health and Medical Research (Inserm, 2014), will end relatively early in a person's life. Others, such as asthma, are less serious and, with the help of effective support, can still maintain a certain quality of life. The sheer number and variety of chronic diseases represent a major challenge for our societies.

According to the Santé Publique France website (InVS, 2014), chronic diseases affect no less than 20% of the population and are one of the major causes of death and disability. We won't provide an exhaustive list of chronic diseases here, but a few figures will illustrate the seriousness of this public health problem. Among the chronic pathologies we find cancer (30% of deaths per year), diabetes, arterial hypertension affecting more than 65% of the over-50s, cardiovascular diseases and obesity, which affects 17% of 18-84 year-olds, again according to the InVS.

Although these figures are significant, they do not always reflect the suffering that can be linked to these diseases and the complications they can cause sufferers. We feel it is important to point out that they also have an impact on the people around them and on relationships, representations, beliefs, behaviour and emotional states (De Clercq, 2013).

In the context of chronic illness, where recovery is no longer an option, healthcare professionals have a duty to help patients continue to live as normally (and with dignity) as possible. Numerous studies and interventions are now pointing the finger at all the factors that can be encouraged, developed and improved so that anyone suffering from a chronic illness can benefit from a quality of life that is sufficient to achieve happiness and well-being.

A.2. Comorbidities

Chronic illness, from the moment it is announced to the end, creates upheaval in the daily lives of sufferers, plunging them momentarily into a state of paralysis (Houlle et al., 2014). Each individual will cope according to their own characteristics and resources, whether internal or external. Faced with this health problem, not everyone will react in the same way. Some, with a wealth of functional internal resources and significant perceived social support, will be able to adjust effectively to the situation (Lazarus and Folkman, 1984) and work to maintain a sufficient quality of life despite the presence of the illness. For others, this ordeal may prove too difficult to manage by their own personal means, and they will require additional support. The most common negative emotions associated with chronic illness are fear, anxiety, depression, helplessness, pessimism and stress (Mikolajczak, 2013).

There are a wide variety of chronic illnesses, yet some, simply by mentioning them, strike a deeper chord. According to the French National Cancer Institute, the estimated number of new cases of cancer in 2017 was 399,500 (214,000 men and 185,500 women) and the estimated number of deaths from cancer was 150,000 (84,000 men and 66,000 women).

The fatalistic representation of cancer, which is very deeply rooted in our society, can have a considerable impact at the time of the announcement, but also throughout the treatment (Pujol, Launay & Boulze, 2012). Some research shows that there are significant levels of anxiety and depression following the diagnosis of cancer (Houlle, Strub, Costantini, Tarquinio & Fischer, 2014). These two factors are described by the authors as potentially constituting vulnerability factors for the emergence of a chronic pathology. In addition, in the case of pathologies that are already established, they can be factors that aggravate symptoms, reduce quality of life and increase the mortality rate (Bayliss, Steiner & Fernald, 2003). Linden, Vodermaier, Mackenzie & Greig (2012), show that following the announcement, 19% of people present anxiety and 12.5% depressive symptoms.

The literature shows that patients with type 2 diabetes who say they are "very stressed" are twice as likely to be depressed (Anderson, Freedland, Clouse & Lustman, 2001). Chronic illness favours a very marked negative affective component, but the reverse can also occur. People with asthma have a higher rate of However, in certain situations, this same anxiety takes the form of a panic attack, which can trigger an asthmatic episode. In these patients, the fear of having such an episode can affect their quality of life by reducing the frequency of activities and increasing emotional distress (Lavoie et al., 2005). The issue of quality of life is going to receive considerable attention in the field of chronic illness, as a major component of patient management.

A.3 Impact on quality of life

According to the WHO (1994), "quality of life refers to an individual's physical health, psychological state, social relationships, level of autonomy and relationship with the essential factors of the environment". This global definition is supplemented by a more specific definition of health. We can define health-related quality of life as "all the subjective perceptions of a patient with regard to his or her physical, emotional and social state in relation to the effects of the disease and treatments" (Fisher & Tarquinio, 2014, p. 10).

Much has now been written and published about the consequences of the potentially restrictive lifestyle imposed by chronic illness. These effects can affect many factors in an individual's life, altering identity, self-representation and body image (Ribes, 2012), as well as self-esteem (Dlugonski & Motl, 2012). In order to compare the quality of life of children and adolescents with chronic illnesses with that of children and adolescents from the general population, Eiser, Eiser and Stride (2005) administered quality of life scales to these two groups. This research revealed that the average scores of the first group were much lower than those of the second. Furthermore, researchers agree that psychological quality of life includes the presence of positive affects, a certain amount of self-confidence, good self-esteem, satisfaction with oneself and one's body image, and a scarcity of negative affects (Bruchon-Schweitzer & Boujut, 2014, p. 50). However, as we have

7

seen above, depression and anxiety are often present, along with chronic illness. According to the DSM-V, the former brings together a set of well-defined symptoms such as depressed mood, anhedonia, abulia, excessive guilt and devaluation as well as significant ruminations which play a central role in maintaining the symptomatology (Nolen-Hoeksema, 2000). We also note in anxiety a strong presence of repetitive thoughts in the form of worries, which are thought to be one of the major factors in generalised anxiety (Borkovec, Alcaine & Behar, 2004). According to Brokovec and his team, ruminations are therefore at the heart of these two disorders.

We therefore wondered whether the quality of life of people suffering from chronic illnesses was not all the more affected when patients report a high level of repetitive negative thoughts, which reinforce the presence of anxiety and depressive symptoms.

B. Ruminations

2.1. The origins of thought

The human brain is in constant activity, producing an almost permanent mental discourse. Harris (2012, p. 146), in one of his books, gives a particularly interesting explanation of our brain's ability to think. Evolution is thought to have given us this ability in the first place, so that we could better apprehend the dangers around us. Thinking would therefore initially have been a powerful survival mechanism, enabling us to assess future prospects on the basis of past dangers, all in order to promote the right behaviour in the present situation. However, while our lives are no longer as much at risk as they were in our former state of nature, we have retained this mental functioning, this willingness to constantly evaluate our experiences, whether internal or external. And in many ways this mechanism is still very favourable. However, this process can also have a much less beneficial aspect. Reminiscence and anticipation are certainly useful, but much less so when they constantly deprive us of the experience of the present. Our judgements are certainly necessary, but much more dangerous when they trap us in a repetitive cycle of self-deprecating thoughts. These cognitions can then be defined as recurrent, prolonged and relatively uncontrollable about our own experiences, whether past, present or future (Watkins, 2008). Some authors have found that this phenomenon of ruminations can be perceived according to different ways of thinking and that the nature of these ways of thinking can have variable effects.

2.2. A dual conceptualisation of thought

Watkins (2008) distinguishes between two types of ruminations. On the one hand, abstract and analytical thoughts (which are non-constructive) and on the other, concrete and experiential thoughts (which are constructive). The former refer to the causes and consequences of the person's condition and the situation in which they find themselves. This mode is the main cognitive driver of depression (Philippot, 2011). The effects of this mode can be seen in a deterioration in mood, or in a reduction in problem-solving abilities, particularly in depressed people (Watkins & Moulds, 2005). The second way of thinking is closer to the experience of a situation at the time it occurs, and would enable realistic and functional attitudes to emerge. Some authors suggest that it is probably this focus on feeling that leads people who use the second mode to improve their emotional process compared with people who use the first (Holmes, Mathews, Dalgleish & MacKintosh 2006).

On the basis of this theory, Watkins, Baeyens & Read (2009) developed a programme of cognitive

8

behavioural therapy focusing on ruminations with dysphoric people. The results show a decrease in the frequency of abstract thoughts and an increase in the use of concrete thoughts. Despite these encouraging results, there is still very little research to show that the intervention had any effect. However, some results tend to show that training in concrete thoughts significantly reduces depressive symptoms compared with an intervention based on relaxation training (Watkins and Moberly, 2009).

2.3. Impact on health

Repetitive negative thoughts, or ruminations, have been the subject of much research, in order to observe their effect on a range of factors linked to individual health (Garnefski, Koopman, Kraaij & Cate, 2009; Kokonyei et al., 2016). According to Holahan et al (In Callahan, S., Chabrol, H., 2013), rumination is defined as a 'passive' but non-avoidant coping strategy that has elements in common with hypervigilance and can be described as rather maladaptive. This type of coping strategy, unlike 'active' coping, refers to inactivity in the face of a stressful event and is often linked to a negative emotional state such as depression (Chabrol & Callahan, 2013). According to other authors (Nolen-Hoeksema, Wisco & Lyubomirsky, 2008), this is a cognitive process that leads people to think negatively about their past, present and future. This rumination is thought to induce significant psychological distress and prevent the use of more functional strategies (Nolen-Hoeksema et al., 1993, in Chabrol & Callahan, 2013). Numerous results have shown that repetitive negative thoughts predict, or even aggravate, the intensity of depressive symptoms (Catteau & Chabrol, 2005) and generalised anxiety (Borkovec & Inz, 1990; Stoeber & Borkovec, 2002; Philippot & Douilliez, 2014), encouraging these two disorders to persist. The more specific experiment by Kraaij et al (2002) shows that depressive symptoms worsen in elderly people with a high ruminations score. A number of authors agree that rumination may be one of the major factors in the development of depressive symptoms (Watkins & Brown, 2002; Nolen-Hoeksema, 2004). Some authors have also linked ruminations to anxiety, and it has been shown that obsessive rumination associated with intrusive thoughts constitutes the first criterion for hypochondria, defined as an anxiety disorder (Tignol, 2014).

The dysfunctional aspect of these repeated and intrusive negative cognitions can go beyond the psychological sphere and also have an impact on the body. Hadijstavropoulos et al (2000) have shown that recurrent thoughts about pain, described as dysfunctional, can increase sensitivity to pain in people with chronic pain.

In the light of the above research, ruminations may indirectly affect quality of life through their role in anxiety and depression symptoms. It would therefore seem appropriate to take this cognitive component into account when supporting people suffering from chronic illness, in order to improve their quality of life.

As we shall see later, interventions based on mindfulness meditation and positive psychology can be judicious therapeutic approaches and tools for reducing the propensity to rumination, developing better emotional management and encouraging the emergence of more effective strategies.

C. Mindfulness

C.l. Definition

Mindfulness is a concept that has come to the fore in recent decades. Although its practical foundations were laid within Buddhist culture, its theoretical aspects have only been investigated over the last forty years.

It is within the third wave of cognitive behavioural therapies (CBTs) that this concept is emerging. This third wave, unlike the first two, focuses on emotions (Teasdale, 2004). It is no longer a question of trying to change our behaviour, our emotions or our thought patterns at all costs, which we would describe as dysfunctional, but of accepting things as they are in order to lessen the impact they may have on us (Kotsou, & Heeren, 2011). We now know that more than our emotions or thoughts themselves, it's the relationship we have with these emotions and thoughts that causes us harm (Phillipot, 2011). So it's not so much a question of fighting back as of accepting our emotional reactions, by adopting a non-judgemental attitude. To clarify the definition of mindfulness, we will quote the definition of the person who has given it its rightful place. Kabat-Zinn (2003), for example, describes the phenomenon of mindfulness (particularly during meditation) as "the act of deliberately paying attention to the internal and external experiences of the present moment without judging them". Mindfulness meditation is therefore an attentional and experiential exercise based on sensory data from our internal climate and information from our environment, where all thoughts and images are welcome.

Based on this concept, numerous interventions have emerged. Jon Kabat-Zinn (1982) was the first to really develop a method he called Mindfulness-Based Stress Reduction (MBSR), which has made it possible to integrate mindfulness meditation into Western medicine. This programme was offered to patients suffering from chronic pain and showed beneficial effects on the experience of pain (Kabat-Zinn, 1982).

From this first programme, many others have developed, such as MBCT (Mindfulness-Based Cognitive Therapy) by Segal, Williams and Teasdale (2006), which works more specifically to reduce depressive symptoms and the risk of depressive relapse; Acceptance and Commitment Therapy (Hayes, Strosahl, Wilson, 1999) and Dialectical Behaviour Therapy (Linehan, 1993). The latter two therapies do not necessarily focus on mindfulness, but mindfulness is a major pillar of their approach.

C.2 Mindfulness at the heart of health

Baer (2003) proposes a quantitative meta-analysis of the effects of mindfulness-based intervention programmes and reveals that the majority of benefits are found in two main areas, namely the reduction of emotional disorders on the one hand, and the reduction of psychological difficulties associated with chronic illness on the other.

With regard to emotional disorders, a number of studies have reported a certain effectiveness of mindfulness training in preventing relapses into depression (Segal, Williams and Teasdale, 2006; Kuyken et al. 2008), in the treatment of recurrent generalised anxiety disorder (Barnhofer et al. 2009) and psychological distress (Brown & Ryan, 2003). Some have also demonstrated a significant effect of mindfulness meditation on reducing ruminations (Raes & Williams, 2010).

Concerning the second axis, i.e. the reduction of psychological difficulties associated with chronic illnesses, an improvement in quality of life has been observed in people suffering from fibromyalgia (Van Gordon, Shonin, Dunn, Garcia-Campayo & Griffiths, 2017), cancer (Chambers et al, 2016), diabetes (Van Son, Nyklicek, Nefs, Speight, Pop & Pouwer, 2015), HIV (Gayneret al., 2012) and multiple sclerosis (Schirda, Nicholas, &Prakash, 2015). All these studies indicate that the benefits of mindfulness training through different interventions based on this concept are mainly found in a reduction in emotional distress, negative affect, anxious thoughts, stress, depressive symptoms and an improvement in sleep and well-being.

Through its effects in reducing negative affect, mindfulness seems to be a tool of great interest for improving patients' experiences. However, as the WHO points out, health is not just the absence of disease, just as mental health is not just the absence of mental pathology or negative affect. A major component of both health and quality of life is the presence of positive emotions. This is where another approach, positive psychology, also finds its place in clinical health psychology.

D. Positive psychology

D.l. What is positive psychology?

According to Gable and Haidt (2005), positive psychology is "the study of the conditions and processes that contribute to the flourishing or optimal functioning of individuals, groups and institutions". Positive psychology was born out of Seligman and Csikszentmihalyi's observation (in Martin-Krumm and Tarquinio, 2011) that, over the last century, psychology and psychological research focused mainly on psychopathology and the study of mental illness and its treatment. The results of this research have made it possible to learn more about human mental functioning and to repair the damage caused by different life courses, particularly those resulting from the atrocities of the wars of the last century (Seligman & Csikszentmihalyi, 2011). Armed with this knowledge, psychologists are able to diagnose and treat many mental disorders. The downside of this development has been to overshadow the other two missions of psychology, namely to make people's lives fuller and more productive, and to identify and develop talent (Seligman, 1994). Seligman and Peterson (2004), through their research into what makes people tick, have contributed to the creation of a list of six major virtues that can be broken down into 24 character strengths and which play a role in our functioning and our ability to be happy (*Cf. Appendix 1*).

The main criticism of positive psychology is that it ignores human suffering. Yet even if positive psychology sets itself the task of studying the conditions and processes that contribute to fulfilment and/or optimal functioning, it nonetheless takes account of people's suffering. Indeed, it might be legitimate to say that research has enabled psychiatrists and psychologists specialising in mental disorders to make considerable progress in the treatment of psychopathologies such as psychosis, anxiety disorders and depression. However, the accumulated knowledge about mental illness and psychopathological disorders has left little room for the development of knowledge about an individual's positive strengths (Seligman, 1994). In recent years, research has attempted to evaluate the effect of these positive strengths on health.

D.2 Positive psychology in the health field

Far from denying the existence of negative emotions, positive psychology focuses on increasing positive emotions. As a reminder, an emotion is a physical and psychological experience associated with a situation or event (Shankland, 2014). Whether positive or negative, emotions have a function. They can inform us about our experience and state through physical manifestations, for example. This information can influence our decisions and attitudes to the situations we encounter. For example, Haase, Poulin and Heckhausen (2012) found that there was a correlation between positive emotions and motivation to overcome obstacles. In addition, individuals expressing positive emotions are said to have more resources available to deal with a problem, and to think more flexibly, more broadly and more creatively (Martin-Krumm and Tarquinio, 2011). Conversely, Boland, Rielage & Hoyt (2017) showed that people who usually express a sad, negative mood were at greater risk of developing a post-traumatic stress episode and of abusing alcohol in response to a stressful event. Other results have highlighted the beneficial effect of positive psychotherapies on depressive symptoms (Seligman, Steen, Park & Peterson, 2005; Seligman, Rashid & Park, 2006; Csillik, Aguerre & Bay, 2012), making them highly complementary to traditional CBT and medication.

Beyond positive emotions, positive psychology places considerable importance on positive dispositions such as resilience, optimism, gratitude and altruism. These dispositions are described as personality traits but also as coping strategies (Shankland, 2014) and a great deal of research has already found their beneficial effects on individuals. For example, it has been found that individuals with a high gratitude score report fewer symptoms of anxiety and depression (Lyubomirsky, 2008), less stress (Shankland, 2010), greater life satisfaction, more optimism and fewer negative emotions (Froh, Sefic & Emmons, 2008), and greater well-being thanks to fewer chronic headaches, digestive problems and sleep disorders.

The notion of well-being refers not only to the presence of positive emotions, but also to the presence of positive cognitions, which also play an important role in this component of health. Indeed, in patients with Parkinson's disease, there is a correlation between positive thoughts and quality of life (Hart, 2016). People who had recently been diagnosed with HIV and had followed a programme based on positive thinking had a much greater positive effect of the treatment than the control group (Moskowitz, 2017). These same groups were also assessed for depressive symptoms. In each group, 17% of people were receiving antidepressant treatment at the start of the intervention. 15 months later, the percentage of people in the experimental group taking antidepressants had not changed, but the percentage had risen to 35% for the control group.

If there is one context in which positive emotions can be impacted, it is the context of illness, particularly chronic illness, which can be a source of multiple emotional disturbances (Moullec, Lavoie & Sultan, 2012). It therefore seems a good idea to invest in this sphere of the positive in order to develop patients' individual resources to improve or maintain their well-being throughout treatment and the illness. To achieve this, programmes based on the theories of positive psychology have been developed. The CARE programme is one example, and it is this that we have chosen to evaluate.

D.3. An example of a positive psychology intervention: the CARE programme

The CARE programme stems from research in the field of positive psychology, and all the exercises presented have a sound theoretical basis (Seligman, Steen, Park and Peterson, 2005).

The programme is aimed at a small group (between 6 and 8 participants) and is based on the third wave of mindfulness interventions. It consists of 8 sessions of around 2 hours each over a total of 8 weeks, with one session per week. The exercises proposed focus on health-protective factors and aim to develop and strengthen individual resources and emotional skills. Through the practical aspect of the exercises, which are repeated throughout the week and from one week to the next, this programme aims to bring about a real change in people's behaviour and experiences, as well as in their relationship with the world and themselves. The main aim of this practice is to redirect attention towards satisfying everyday events, to identify and strengthen character strengths and to develop commitment to meaningful actions (Shankland, André & Kotsou, 2015). The exercises also aim to encourage

increased resilience, feelings of gratitude, optimism, altruism and self-esteem. These are all factors that contribute to people's quality of life (Martin-Krumm & Tarquinio, 2011, p.431).

E. Issues and general hypotheses

E.l. Issues and hypotheses

The question of quality of life in chronic illness is central. In this study, we will attempt to observe an improvement in quality of life through the development of certain emotional, cognitive and behavioural skills, as well as a reduction in abstract and analytical ruminations, which are defined as non-constructive and often deleterious, via two interventions based on distinct theoretical models (CARE and MBI). Although they differ in content, these two approaches have elements in common. Whether the programmes are based on mindfulness meditation or positive psychology, each focuses on personality traits that can improve emotional well-being (empathy, acceptance, self-regulation, emotional expression, trust, gratitude), cognitive well-being (psychological flexibility, redirection of attention, openness) and behavioural well-being (engagement in meaningful actions). Our question is how these two programmes might influence the quality of life of chronic patients. What differences in effect, if any, would we find between the two groups?

There are many reasons for this study. On the one hand, it would highlight the relevance of interventions based on mindfulness and positive psychology with chronically ill patients, in order to improve their experience. Secondly, depending on the results obtained, we would like to encourage the introduction of this type of group intervention in the public sector, in order to reach as many people as possible.

Our assumptions:

Hl: The programme based on mindfulness meditation and the positive psychology programme improve participants' quality of life.

H2: The mindfulness meditation programme and the positive psychology programme reduce anxiety-depressive symptoms

H3: The mindfulness meditation programme and the positive psychology programme reduce the frequency of abstract and analytical thoughts

Our operational assumptions :

HO1: SF-36 scores will be significantly higher for both groups in Time 2 than in Time 1.

HO2: The mean HADS scores for anxiety and depression will be significantly lower for both groups in Time 2 than in Time 1.

HO3 : The mean scores obtained in the Mini-Certs were significantly lower for the abstract analytical thoughts dimension at time 2 than at time 1, for both groups. And the mean scores obtained for the concrete experiential thoughts dimension were significantly higher at time 2 than at time 1, for both groups.

CHAPTER 3

III.   Methods

A. Participants

The participants were selected from the Bordeaux University Hospital Centre's Medical Specialties Unit. They are patients who are regularly monitored in the tropical and infectious diseases and rheumatology departments.

For this research, we only took patients whose pathology had stabilised and who were willing to complete the various questionnaires at Time 1 (start of intervention) and Time 2 (end of intervention). The participants were referred by the referring psychologist or by the ward doctors.

The inclusion criteria are the presence of a chronic illness and follow-up in the above-mentioned services. Exclusion criteria are the presence of a major mood disorder previously assessed by the referring psychologist.

Table 1: Characteristics of the study population (N=8)

	Group	Age	Gender	Pathology
Participant 1	CARE	46	H	HIV
Participant 2	CARE	29	F	Rheumatoid arthritis
Pathology 3	CARE	62	F	Diabetes
Participant 4	CARE	64	H	HIV + cardiovascular disease
Participant 5	MBI	88	F	Wegner's disease
Participant 6	MBI	57	F	Fibromyalgia
Participant 7	MBI	53	F	HIV
Participant 8	MBI	58	F	Cancer of the tonsil

The study involved a total of 8 participants: 4 participants in the MBI programme and 4 participants in the CARE programme. The average age for the CARE group was 50.25 (SD = 14.11) and 64 (SD = 13.98) for the MBI group. The majority of participants in the study were women (75%).

The participants were received individually by the trainee psychologist so that the research protocol could be explained to them. A minimum level of commitment was also required in order to be able to really report on the effects of the interventions (participants had to attend at least 7 out of the 8 sessions). It was during these interviews that the first tests were administered.

The experimental groups are run by three instructors. Two psychologist instructors lead the mindfulness programme and one instructor leads the CARE programme (psychologist trainee).

B. Tests used

• We used the MOS SF-36 by Ware and Sherboume (92; translated into French by Leplege, Ecosse, Verdier & Perneger, 1998), which assesses health status independently of disease and provides a generic score for evaluating quality of life. We chose it for its multidimensional aspect, as the SF-36 assesses 8 components of health status, including perceived health, relationships with others, and physical and psychological health.

14

The SF-36 has very good psychometric qualities (sensitivity, internal consistency, test-retest reliability) and is undoubtedly the most widely used generic quality of life scale.

• To assess repetitive thoughts our choice fell on the French and brief version of the Cambridge-Exeter Repetitive Thought Scale (mini-CERTS) by Douillez et al. (2014). The questionnaire assesses repetitive thoughts along two dimensions: abstract analytic thoughts (AAP) and concrete experiential thoughts (CEP). Although the validation article reveals a weak sensitivity of the tool, the rest of its psychometric qualities remain sufficiently reliable to make it an interesting scale. The minimum score is 8 and the maximum 32 for each dimension of the questionnaire.

• Finally, we opted for the Hospital Anxiety Depression Scale (HADS) by Zigmond & Snaith (1983, translated into French by Lépine in 1985) to assess anxiety-depressive symptoms. We chose it because it is quick to administer and can assess both components (anxiety and depression). To screen for anxiety and depressive symptoms, the scores per dimension will be evaluated as follows:

- 7 or less: no symptoms
- 8 to 10: dubious symptoms
- 11 and over: definite symptoms

C. Experimental protocol

C.1. Description of the Mindfulness programme

The mindfulness or MBI (Mindfulness Based Intervention) programme is based on the MBSR model by Kabat-Zin (1982) and the MBCT model by Segal, Teasdale and Williams (2006). Its aim is to introduce participants to the practice of mindfulness meditation through exercises, formal practices (body-scan, breath meditation, sitting meditation) and informal practices (practices in everyday life). Some of the exercises have been adapted to suit people with chronic pain. For example, the body scan, which initially lasts 45 minutes, has been reduced to 25-30 minutes. Several sessions also focus on identifying thought patterns, cognitions and emotions. The instructors also included psycho-education and a theoretical input on mindfulness meditation in the health sector. (*See Appendix 2*)

The programme consists of one two-hour session a week for 8 weeks, with practice sessions to be carried out at home between each session.

C.2 Description of the CARE programme

The aim of the CARE positive psychology programme (Shankland, Kotsou and André, 2015) is to develop greater psychological flexibility by changing attitudes and habitual automatic behaviours. This objective is broken down into three main areas:

- Redirecting attention towards the satisfying aspects of everyday life, whether it's about oneself, one's interactions or outside oneself (others, the environment).
- Develop a caring, non-judgmental attitude towards yourself, others and the environment.
- Develop commitment to actions that correspond to your values and fundamental psychological needs, such as the need for social connection, a sense of competence and autonomy. This last point in the programme is essential.

For example, the CARE programme offers the 3 satisfying events exercise (Seligman et al., 2005), the gratitude

15

letter and the *Values In Action* questionnaire on the internet. In addition, a theoretical aspect is provided on the various major concepts of the positive psychology and health psychology approach: self-kindness, resilience, gratitude, coping strategies. (*Cf. Appendix 3*)

The rhythm of the programme follows that of the mindfulness programme, i.e. one 2-hour session per week over 8 weeks, with individual practice between each session.

CHAPTER 4

IV. RESULTS Results

A. Descriptive analysis

To present the results, we will begin by describing the statistics for the CARE group, then those for the MBI group, and finally we will attempt to compare the results between the two groups. To do this, we will use the various graphs presented below.

Graph 1: Average scores for the CARE group on the different scales in Periods 1 and 2

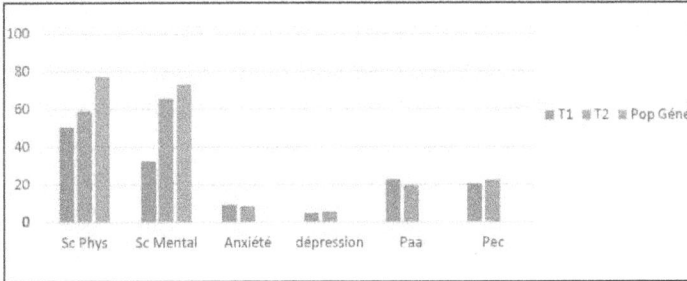

Paa: Abstract analytical thoughts / Pec: Concrete experiential thoughts. T1 Time 1 / T2=Time 2 Sc Phys: Physical score / Sc Mental: Mental score

Notes: *for information only, we have chosen to show the mean of the physical and mental scores obtained on the SF-36 in the general population (in grey) in order to better reflect any differences with our experimental population (Leplège, Ecosse, Verdier & Perneger, 1998).*

In the CARE group, the mean scores for the Physical and Mental dimensions of the SF-36 appear to differ between time 1 and time 2. The difference is particularly noticeable in the Mental score. The Physical score of the test was 50.28 (o =23.10) at T1 compared with 58.90 (o =22.94) at T2. The Mental score was T1=32.31 (o=15.77) compared with T2=65.45 (o=5.48). The standard deviation obtained for the Mental dimension at time 1 was high, revealing that there was considerable variation in the data. For the other scales, we found slight variations at T1 and T2 for the Anxiety and PAA scores.

Graph 2: Average scores for the MBI group on the various scales in Periods 1 and 2

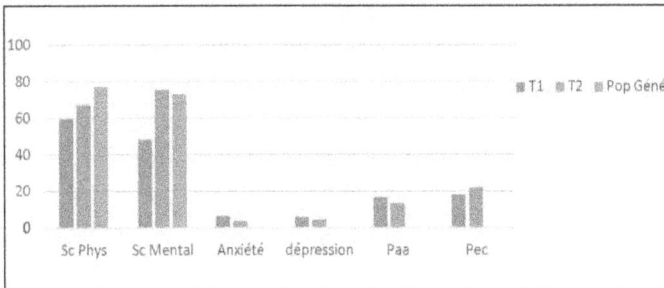

In the MBI group, there was a difference in the SF-36 Mental score between T1=48.33 (o=4.41) and T2=64.16 (o=21.46). There were slight variations at T1 and T2 in the Physical, Anxiety, Depression, PAA and PEC scores.

17

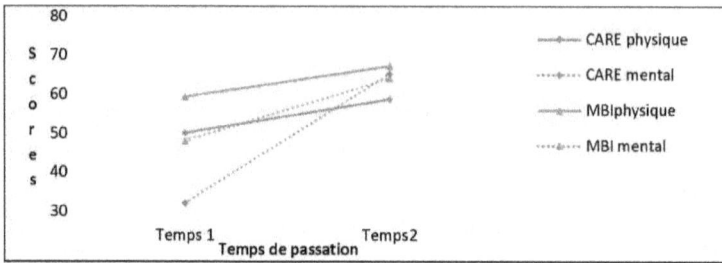

The curves show an increasing trend in the mean scores for each group and for each dimension of the SF-36 between time 1 and time 2.

Graph 4: Average HADS scores for the CARE and MBI groups at times 1 and 2

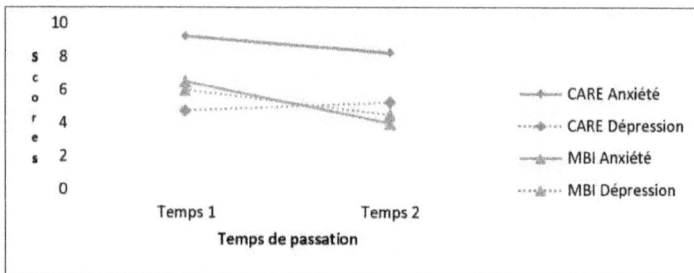

We can see above a downward trend between T1 and T2 for the Anxiety score for both groups. This trend is also observed for the Depression score, but only for the MBI group.

Graph 5: Average scores of the CARE and MBI groups in the Mini-Certs at times 1 and 2

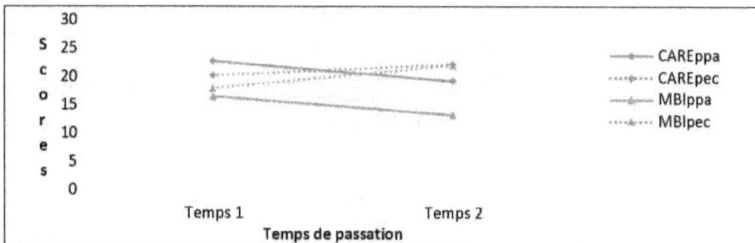

Graph 5 shows an upward trend in PEC scores between T1 and T2 and a downward trend in PAA scores between T1 and T2 for both groups.

B. Statistical analysis

For the statistical treatment of our study, we had to use the non-parametric version of the Student's t test. In fact, it did not seem relevant to us to test the normality of the distributions on such small samples (CARE N=4 and MBI N=4), since normality tests, in this type of case, are insufficiently powerful to allow the null hypothesis to be rejected (Broc, 2016., p.210). As a result, they tend to return a systematically positive result in terms of normality and homogeneity. We therefore opted to use the non-parametric Wilcoxon median comparison test. We could have obtained a more relevant analysis if the samples had been larger, allowing us to use parametric tests. We are aware that non-parametric tests are often more severe, more conservative, and

18

give a higher p-value, which may lead to slightly different results compared with those obtained with parametric tests. It should be noted that we carried out a dispersion test on our data, which ensured that there were no outliers (*Cf. Appendix 4*).

CARE group vs MBI group at Time 1

Table 2: Comparison of CARE and MBI group scores at time 1

Variables measured	Group averages (*standard deviation*) Medians		Significance .... Value of *p*
	CARE	MBI	
Physical score	50,28 *(23,10)* 55,50	59,51 *(19,91)* 66,12	0.4857 ns
Mental score	32,31 *(15,77)* 64,50	48,33 *(4,41)* 47,05	0.0571 ns
Anxiety score	9,25 *(7,80)* 7	6,50 *(0,58)* 6,50	1 ns
Depression score	4,75 *(4,11)* 4,50	6 *(2,16)* 6,50	0.6857 ns
Paa	22,75 *(9,60)* 23,50	16,50 *(2,89)* 16,50	0.6592 ns
Pec	20,25 *(3,59)* 19,50	18 *(5,29)* 17	0.5614 ns

Paa: abstract analytical thoughts /Pec: Concrete experiential thoughts /Ns: not significant

Notes *: For ease of reading and understanding, we have kept the score averages in our tables, but bear in mind that the associated p-value was calculated on the medians and not the averages.*

We compared the medians of the CARE group with those of the MBI group at time 1 to ensure that there was no significant difference between our two samples. Here, the test reveals no significant difference between our two samples (*Table 2*). The medians are therefore not significantly different (p>.05 for each scale).

CARE group Time 1 vs Time 2

Tableau 3 Comparison of the average scores of the Care group on the different scales in Time 1 and Time 2

Variables measured	Care Group averages (standard deviation) Medians		Significance
	T1	T2	Value of *p*
Physical score	50,28 *(23,10)* 55,5	58,90 *(22,94)* 72,5	0.1003 ns
Mental score	32,31 *(15,77)* 64,5	65,45 *(5,48)* 70,69	0.1003 ns
Anxiety score	9,25 *(7,80)* 7	8,25 *(5,91)* 3	0.7127 ns
Depression score	4,75 *(4,11)* 4,5	5,25 *(2,22)* 4,5	0.8551 ns
Paa	22,75 *(9,60)* 23,5	19,25 *(8,50)* 12	0.097 ns
Pec	20,25 *(3,59)* 19,5	22,25 *(1,50)* 22	0.461 ns

Although we note some differences between the mean scores at T1 and T2 for the Physical score (T1=50.28 vs T2=58.90) but especially for the Mental score (T1 = 32.31 vs T2 = 65.45), the Wilcoxon paired-samples test reveals no significant difference (p > .05). If we consider the analysis of the data presented above, it would appear that the CARE group intervention did not bring any significant improvement for the dimensions physical score, mental score, anxiety, depression, abstract analytical thoughts and concrete experiential thoughts.

Notes : For a more detailed graphical overview of the evolution of the CARE group's scores on the SF-36 sub-dimensions between time 1 and time 2, see Appendix 5.

MBI group Time 1 vs. Time 2

Tableau 4   Comparison of the mean scores of the MBI group on the different scales in Time 1 and Time 2

Variables measured	MBI group averages *(standard deviation)* Medians				Significance
	T1		T2		Value of *p*
Physical score	59,51	*(19,91)* 66,12	67,42	*(23,39)* 72,5	0.8551	ns
Mental score	48,33	*(4,41)* 47,05	64,16	*(21,46)* 70,69	0,2012	ns
Anxiety score	6,50	*(0,58)* 6,5	4	*(2,71)* 3	0,1975	ns
Depression score	6	*(2,16)* 6,5	4,50	*(2,38)* 4,5	0.5862	ns
Paa	16,50	*(2,89)* 16,5	13,25	*(2,50)* 12	0,1003	ns
Pec	18	*(5,29)* 17	22	*(5,23)* 22	0,1003	ns

Notes : For a more detailed graphical overview of the evolution of the CARE group's scores on the SF-36 sub-dimensions between time 1 and time 2, see Appendix 6.

In the same way as for the previous group, we note a change in the mean scores in several dimensions at T1 and T2. Table 4 shows higher mean scores for the Physical score (T1 = 59.51 vs T2 = 67.42), Mental score (T1=48.33 vs T2=64.16) and PEC (T1=18 vs T2 =22) dimensions. There was a decrease in the mean scores for Anxiety (T1=6.50 vs T2=4) and Depression (T1=6 vs T2=4.50). However, the Wilcoxon test revealed no significant change for each variable measured (p > .05).

As with the CARE group, based on the results obtained after statistical analysis, we can suggest that the intervention of the MBI group had no significant effect on our sample in each of the dimensions measured.

CARE group vs. MBI group at Time 2

Table 5: Comparison of CARE and MBI group scores at time 2

Variables measured	Group averages *(standard deviation)* Medians				Significance .... Value of *p*
	CARE		MBI		
Physical score	58,90	*(22,94)* 72,5	67,42	*(23,39)* 62,80	0.4857 ns
Mental score	65,45	70,69	64,16	64,50	0.6857 ns
Anxiety score	8,25	*(5,91)* 3	4	*(2,71)* 6	0.1886 ns
Depression score	5,25	*(2,22)*	4,50	*(2,38)*	

	4,50	6	*0.8809 ns*
Paa	19,25 12	13,25　*(2,50)* 19	*0.4596 ns*
Pec	22,25　*(1,50)* 22	22　　*(5,23)* 22	1 ns

To complete this statistical analysis, we compared the scores of our two groups at T2.

We can see some differences in the means. The mean score for the Physical score dimension is higher at T2 for the MBI group (m=67.42) compared to the CARE group (m=58.90). Similarly, the Anxiety score is lower at T2 for the MBI group (m=4) compared to the CARE group (m=8.25). We also see a lower mean PAA score for the MBI group (m=13.25) compared to the CARE group (m=19.25).

The differences in means suggest that the MBI intervention had a greater effect on the Physical score, Anxiety, and PAA dimensions than the CARE intervention. But, once again, the Wilcoxon test indicates no significant difference between our two samples at T2 for all scales (p >.05). We cannot therefore conclude that one group was more effective than the other, whatever the dimensions assessed.

To sum up

In view of the results of the comparative analyses, we cannot reject our null hypotheses according to which there would be no significant differences in the scores obtained by our two groups at T1 and T2 for the SF-36, HADS and Mini-Certs scales. Indeed, we find that none of our operational hypotheses is confirmed.

We cannot therefore conclude that the CARE Group intervention had a significant beneficial effect on the quality of life, anxiety-depressive symptomatology and ruminations of our sample. Similarly, we cannot conclude that the MBI Group's intervention had a significant beneficial effect on the quality of life, anxiety-depressive symptomatology and ruminations of our sample.

CHAPTER 5

V. Discussion

The aim of our research was to evaluate the effect of two distinct groups, the mindfulness group (MBI) and the positive psychology group (CARE), on a population of chronically ill patients, by targeting several factors, namely quality of life, anxiety and depressive symptoms, and ruminations. The idea of introducing these interventions was developed on the basis of observations of the problems encountered on the training sites, discussions with other healthcare professionals and the literature.

With regard to the results obtained from the SF-36, the mean scores seem to corroborate the information found in the literature. The MBI group presented a Tl=59.5l score for the Physical dimension and a Tl=48.33 score for the Mental dimension. The CARE group had a Tl score of 50.28 on the Physical dimension and a Tl score of 32.31 on the Mental dimension. If we compare the mean scores obtained in the general population (Leplège, Scotland, Verdier & Perneger, 1998), Physical score = 77.6 and Mental score = 72.7, the latter turn out to be higher. However, we cannot state that they are significantly different. On the other hand, statistical analysis indicates that the interventions do not appear to have had the desired effect on quality of life, contrary to the data we found in the literature (Sin & Lyubomirsky, 2009; Hu & Gruber, 2008).

Numerous studies confirm that chronic illness can be accompanied by comorbid mood disorders (Linden, Vodermaier, Mackenzie, Greig, 2012). Here the CARE group score reveals questionable anxiety symptomatology (m=9.25 >7) but no depressive symptomatology (m=4.75 <7). We note, however, that this depression score is higher than T2 (5.25), which does not seem to corroborate the data found on the benefits of positive psychology in reducing depressive symptoms (Sin & Lyubomirsky, 2009). Note that this difference was not significant (p=.07) and therefore cannot be taken into consideration. In the MBI group, the mean HADS scores revealed neither anxiety (m=6.50 <7) nor depression (M=6 <7). Although we found lower means for both dimensions at T2 (Anxiety=4 and Depression=4.50), compared with T1, we cannot conclude that there was a real effect of the intervention in the absence of significant results.

It should be remembered that our aim was not to compare the effectiveness of the two interventions, but to observe differences in the effect of the two interventions on our measured variables.

An inter-group statistical analysis was also performed. As with the within-group analysis, there were no significant differences in the SF-36, HADS or Mini-Certs scores between the two groups at T1 and T2. The fact that there was no significant difference in the scores of the two groups at T1 is reassuring, showing that the participants in the two groups were probably correctly selected and that the samples were equivalent. Nevertheless, it can be noted that the mean score obtained by the CARE group on the Anxiety dimension of the HADS is associated with doubtful symptomatology (9.25 > 7) compared with the mean score obtained by the MBI group, which is associated with an absence of symptomatology (6.50<7).

In terms of our results, this research was unable to confirm our hypotheses. It would appear that the two interventions had no particular effect on our participants' quality of life, anxiety and depressive symptoms, or thoughts about the future.

repetitive thoughts. Nevertheless, we can see from the graph that there was a trend towards an improvement in quality of life and the use of concrete experiential thoughts for both groups. We also note a downward trend

22

in anxiety and depression levels (except for the level of depression in the CARE group) and in the use of abstract analytical thoughts for both groups. However, these trends were not highlighted by the statistical tests, and we are therefore very cautious about these observations. These remarks should not be taken as anything other than encouragement for future research into these results.

We have attempted to identify the factors inherent in our research that could explain the absence of any significant effect of our interventions. These factors constitute the weaknesses of this study, but also its limitations.

First of all, we would like to highlight the individual feedback received from the participants concerning their level of personal practice between each session. A number of participants said that they did little or nothing to complete the weekly tasks and exercises. Yet it is this aspect of daily practice, which admittedly requires a certain amount of discipline, which is a vector of real and possible benefits (Segal, Williams & Teasdale, 2002). The introduction of motivational interviews prior to the sessions, focusing on the implementation of the intention, could perhaps have strengthened the motivation to practise between sessions (Miller & Rollnick, 2013).

A number of participants told us that they had undergone a number of medical examinations over the eight weeks, had experienced attacks of acute pain and had had to change their treatment as a result. This may have had an impact on their commitment to daily exercise. Unfortunately, these parasite variables had not been taken into account and may have had an effect on our results.

As highlighted in the literature, patients with chronic illness can suffer emotional repercussions in the form of anxious or depressive symptomatology (Houlle et al., 2014). According to the DSM-5, one of the components of depressed mood is a loss of motivation resulting in a loss of interest (anhedonia) and difficulty performing activities. However, the mean HADS scores for the CARE group and the MBI group do not seem to indicate the presence of a proven depressive symptomatology. Our results therefore do not allow us to link the lack of weekly exercise with any depressive symptoms.

One major aspect that may also explain the low effectiveness found in our statistical analyses is undoubtedly the small size of our sample (n=4 for each group). A larger number of participants might have revealed a greater effect. To this we would also add the lack of a control group, which constituted a considerable bias in our comparison of scores. We would have liked to set up a waiting group which would have benefited from the intervention at a later date. Although this was an interesting prospect, it was not possible for logistical reasons and lack of time, nor was it possible to evaluate the effects of our interventions over the longer term. We would have liked to be able to evaluate the progress of our participants' practice three and then six months after the intervention. In addition, we would have found it relevant to evaluate a biological marker of the disease in order to observe the physiological effect of our intervention. For reasons of authorisation, we were unable to set up such an evaluation.

We also note our lack of training as instructors as a factor that may have affected the effectiveness of our intervention. In fact, our knowledge and know-how as group facilitators are largely based on our own reading and experiences as participants in these groups, which may have had an impact on their effectiveness but also on the legitimacy of my work as perceived by the participants. Similarly, for the MBI group, it was

23

the first time that the two psychologists had worked together, and for one of them it was also her first experience as a mindfulness group leader. We can suggest that these different variables may have influenced the effect of the interventions.

We are also aware that the fact that the researcher and the instructor are the same person could pose a problem and we have considered this aspect as a limitation to our research. This last point raises our attention because of its double aspect. Indeed, as we have indicated, the fact that the researcher and the instructor are the same person can be a limitation. However, in the context of this study, we felt it was also relevant to see it as an asset. Indeed, it seems to us that our role as researchers here is to look at our statistical results in order to assess whether or not our action has had a significant effect. From this simple perspective, we can see that, in this action-research project, the interventions did not have a significant effect.

significant. However, as clinicians and instructors, we have seen a great deal of feedback on the changes reported by participants and on the perceived benefits (real or otherwise). We felt it was important to clarify this last point to encourage future action in this area.

CHAPTER 6

VI.   Conclusion

Chronic diseases are many and varied, and their number is increasing every year, affecting more and more people and their families. This makes them a major public health problem. The cognitive, affective and behavioural disturbances that can result from being chronically ill mean that psychological care can be a particularly important and beneficial asset in reducing the impact of these disturbances. There are many different types of psychological intervention in the healthcare field (CBT, emotion regulation therapy, psychoanalysis, motivational interviewing, etc.), but the main aim is to support patients and provide them with the keys they need to regain or maintain a certain quality of life, despite the presence of the disease.

In this action-research project, we chose to focus on two types of approach when selecting our interventions: positive psychology and mindfulness meditation. Our two interventions did not have the desired effect and our hypotheses were not validated. We found no significant effect of our two interventions on the variables Quality of life, Anxiety, Depression and Ruminations. Our results do not corroborate those found in the literature and must be taken into consideration in the light of the many weaknesses and limitations mentioned above.

Nevertheless, all the observations and reflections made by this work, and shared by all the professionals involved in the programmes, have confirmed that these two theoretical approaches are highly complementary. The literature also tells us about the very recent development of a programme combining the two approaches, Ivtzan's Positive Mindfulness Program (PMP) (2016), which suggests interesting prospects for research and validation for the future of psychology in the healthcare sector.

CHAPTER 7

VII. References

1. Anderson, R. J., Freedland, K. E., Clouse, R. E. & Lustman, P. J. (2001). The prevalence of comorbid depression in adults with diabetes. A meta-analysis. *Diabetes care*, 24, 1069-1078.

2. Angel, P., Marteau, F. & Lecomte, J. (2014). Chapter 6. Positive psychology: a new impetus for psychotherapy? In *Introduction to positive psychology* (pp. 93-106). Paris: Dunod. doi:10.3917/dunod.lecom.2014.01.0093.

3. Antonaci, F., Nappi, G., Galli, F., Manzoni, G. C., Calabresi, P. & Costa, A. 2011). Migraine and psychiatric comorbidity: A review of clinical findings. *The Journal ofHeadache and Pain*, 12, 115-125.

4. Baer, R. A. (2003). Mindfulness training as a clinical intervention: A conceptual and empirical review. In Kotsou, I. & Heeren, A. (2011). *Mindfulness and acceptance: Third wave therapies.* Louvain-la-Neuve, Belgium: De Boeck Supérieur.

5. Barnard, P., Watkins, E., Mackintosh, B. & Nimmo-Smith, I. (2007). *Getting stuck in a mental rut: Some process and experiential attributes.* Paper presented at the 35th congress of the British Association for Behavioural and Cognitive Psychotherapies, Brighton, England.

6. Bayliss E. A., Steiner J. F., Fernald D. H. (2003). Description of barriers to self-care by persons with comorbid chronic diseases, *The Annals of Family Medicine*, 1, 15-21.

7. Beaumont, L., de Fays, L., Dermience, E., Gobert, P., Gueibe, P., Poncelet, C., Servais, N. & Verhelle, A. (2013). Chapitre 4. Les migraines. In *Les interventions en psychologie de la santé* (pp. 65-84). Paris: Dunod. doi:10.3917/dunod.mikol.2013.01.0065.

8. Berghmans C., (2011). Chapter 20: Mindfulness and positive psychology. In *Traité de psychologie positive.* Louvain-la-Neuve, Belgium: De Boeck Supérieur.

9. Boland, M., Rielage, J. K., & Hoyt, T. (2017). The Power of Negative Mood in PredictingPosttraumatic Stress Disorder and Alcohol Abuse Comorbidity. *Psychological Trauma: Theory, Research, Practice, And Policy,*

10. Boonstra A.M., Reneman M.F., Stewart R.E.W., Schiphorst Preuper H.R. (2013). Life satisfaction in patients with chronic musculoskeletal pain and its predictors. *QualLife Res.* 22: 93-101. 10.1007/s11136-012-0132-8.

11. Borkovec, T.D. & Inz, J. (1990). The nature of wony in generalized anxiety disorder: A predominance of thought activity. *Behaviour Research and Therapy, 28*, 153-158.

12. Borkovec, T. D., Alcaine, O., & Behar, E. (2004). Avoidance theory of wony and generalized anxiety disorder. In R. G. Heimberg, C. L. Turk & D. S. Mennin (Eds), *Generalized anxiety disorder: Advances in research and practice* (pp. 77-108). New York, USA: Guilford Press.

13. Bruchon-Schweitzer, M. & Boujut, É. (2014). Happiness, life satisfaction, well-being, health and quality of life. In *Psychologie de la santé: Concepts, méthodes et modèles (*pp. 3-82). Paris: Dunod.

14. Callahan, S., Chabrol, H. (2013). *Defence mechanisms and coping.* Paris: Dunod.

15. Carricaburu, D. & Ménoret, M. (2004). Chapter 6 - Chronic illness and normalisation. In
   A. Carricaburu & M. Ménoret (Dir), *Sociologie de la santé: Institutions, professions et maladies* (pp.

91106). Paris: Armand Colin.

16. Catteau V., Chabrol H. (2005). "Étude des relations entre les stratégies d'adaptation aux sentiments dépressifs, la symptomatologie dépressive et les idées suicidaires chez l'adolescent", *L'Année psychologique, 105* ,451-476.

17. Csillik A., Aguerre C. & Bay M. (2012). Positive psychotherapy of depression: specialties and clinical contributions. *Annales Médico-psychologiques, psychiatric journal.* Vol 170, 541-546.

18. Chambers, S. K., Foley, E., Clutton, S., McDowall, R., Occhipinti, S., Berry, M., & ... Smith, D. P. (2016). The role of mindfulness in distress and quality of life for men with advanced prostate cancer. *Quality Of Life Research: An International Journal Of Quality Of Life Aspects Of Treatment, Care & Rehabilitation, 25*(12), 3027-3035.

19. Clifton, D. O. (1997). The Self-Reflection Scale. In Fisher, G-N., & Tarquinio C., (2014). *Health psychology.* Applications et interventions. Paris, Dunod.

20. Cottraux, J. (2012). *Positive psychology and well-being at work.* Paris, Elsevier-Masson.

21. De Clercq, A., de Tender, É., de Thomaz de Bossière, C., Flas, A., Moeyaert, A., Thibaut, A. & Vandeberg, A. (2013). Chapter 3. Chronic low back pain. In *Les interventions en psychologie de la santé* (pp. 41-63). Paris: Dunod. doi:10.3917/dunod.mikol.2013.01.0041.

22. Dlugonski D., Motl R.W. (2012). Possible antecedents and consequences of self-esteem in persons with multiple sclerosis: Preliminary evidence from a cross-sectional analysis, *Rehabilitation Psychology*, 57, 1, 35-42.

23. Douilliez, C., Heeren, A., Lefebvre, N., Watkins, E., Barnard, P. & Philippot, P. (2011). *A brief questionnaire assessing repetitive constructive and non-constructive thoughts. Manuscript submitted for publication.*

24. DSM-5, Diagnostic *and* Statistical Manual *of Mental Disorders,* published by *the American Psychiatric Association* in 2013.

25. Eiser, C., Eiser, J.R., Stride, C.B. (2005). Quality of Life in Children newly diagnosed with Cancer and their Mother. In Bruchon-Schweitzer, M. & Boujut, É. (2014). *Health psychology: Concepts, methods and models* (pp. 3-82). Paris: Dunod.

26. Elliot, T., Renier, C. & Palcher, A.J. (2003). Chronic Pain, Depression, and Quality of Life: Correlations and Predictive Value of the SF-36, *Pain Medicine*, Volume 4, Issue 4, 1, Pages 331- 339, https://doi.org/10.1111/j.1526-4637.2003.03040.x

27. Erpelding, M. L., Boini, S., Fagot-Campagna, A., Mesbah, M., Chwalow, J., Penfornis, A. (2009). Quality of life reference values (DHP) in people with diabetes living in France - Entred 2001-2003. *Bulletin Epidémiologique Hebdomadaire*, 34, 368-371.

28. Fischer, G. & Tarquinio, C. (2014). Chapter 1. Health psychology: the conceptual framework. In G. Fischer & C. Tarquinio (Dir), *The fundamental concepts of health psychology* (pp. 7-27). Paris: Dunod.

29. Froh, J. J., Sefick, W. J., & Emmons, R. A. (2008). Counting blessings in early adolescents: An experimental study of gratitude and subjective well-being. *Journal ofSchool Psychology,* 46(2), 213233. doi: 10.1016/j.jsp.2007.03.005

30. Galand, C. & Salès-Wuillemin, É. (2009). Apports de l'étude des représentations sociales dans le domaine de la santé. Sociétés, 105,(3), 35-44. doi:10.3917/soc.105.0035.

31. Garnefski, N., Koopman, H., Kraaij, V. & Cate, R. (2009). Brief report: Cognitive emotion regulation strategies and psychological adjustment in adolescents with a chronic disease. *Journal of Adolescence*, Volume 32, Issue 2,

32. Gayner, B., Esplen, M. J., DeRoche, P., Wong, J., Bishop, S., Kavanagh, L., & Butler, K. (2012). A randomized controlled trial of mindfulness-based stress reduction to manage affective symptoms and improve quality of life ingay men living with HIV. *Journal Of BehavioralMedicine, 35*(3), 272-285.

33. Harris, R. (2012). *Switch to ACT: Practical acceptance and commitment therapy.* (Penet, C., Milleville, L.) Louvain-la-Neuve, Belgium: De Boeck Supérieur. doi:10.3917/dbu.harri.2012.01.

34. Hayes, S. C., Strosahl, K., Wilson, K. G. (1999). *Acceptance and commitment therapy: an experiential approach to behavior change.* New York: Guilford Press.

35. Holahan C.J., Moos R.J., Holahan C.K., Brennan P.L., Schutte K.K., (2005). "Stress generation, avoidance coping and depressive symptoms: A 10-year model. In Callahan, S., Chabrol, H. (2013). *Mécanismes de défense et coping.* Paris: Dunod.

36. Holmes, E. A., Mathews, A., Dalgleish, T., & Mackintosh, B. (2006). Positive interpretation training: effects of mental imagery versus verbal training on positive mood. *Behavior Therapy, 37*, 237-247.

37. Houlle, W., Strub, L., Costantini, M., Tarquinio, C. & Fischer, G. (2014). Chapter 5. The contributions of psychotherapies in health and illness. In *Psychologie de la santé: applications et interventions* (pp. 109-148). Paris: Dunod.

38. Hu, J. & Gruber, K. (2008). Positive and negative affect and health functionning indicators in older adults with chronic illness. *Issues in Mental Health Nursing, 29*, 895-911

39. Hurt, C. S., Bum, D. J., Hindle, J., Samuel, M., Wilson, K., & Brown, R. G. (2014). Thinking positively about chronic illness: An exploration of optimism, illness perceptions and well-being in patients with Parkinson's disease. *British Journal Of Health Psychology, 19*(2), 363-379.

40. Inserm (2014). *Mucoviscidosis: Encouraging therapeutic avenues.* Retrieved from Inserm website: https://www.inserm.fr/information-en-sante/dossiers-information/mucoviscidose

41. Ivtzan, I., Young, T., Martman, J., Jeffrey, A., Lomas, T., Hart, R., & Eiroa-Orosa, F. J. (2016). Integrating mindfulness into positive psychology: A randomised controlled trial of an online positive mindfulness program. *Mindfulness.* http://dx.doi.org/10.1007/s12671-016-0581-1

42. Kabat-Zinn, J. (1982). An outpatient program in behavioral medicine for chronic pain patients based on the practice of mindfulness meditation: theoretical considerations and preliminary results. *General Hospital Psychiatry, 4*, 33-47.

43. Kabat-Zinn, J., Massion, A. O., Kristeller, J., Peterson, L. G., Fletcher, K. E., Pbert, L., et al (1992). Effectiveness of a meditation-based stress reduction program in the treatment of anxiety disorders. American Journal of Psychiatry, 149, 936-943.

44. Kabat-Zinn, J. (2003). Mindfulness-based intervention in context: past, present and future. *Clinical Psychology: Science and Practice, 10*, 144-156.

45.Kraaij V., Pruymboom E., Garneski N. (2002). "Cognitive Coping and Depressive Symptoms in the Elderly: A Longitudinal Study, *Aging and Mental Health, 6* (3), 275-281.

46.Kokonyei, G., Szabo,E., Kocsel, N., Edes, A., Eszlari, N., Pap, D., Magyar, M., Kovacs, D., Zsombok, T., Elliott, R., Anderson, I.A., Deakin,J.F.W., Bagdy, G. & Juhasz, G. (2016) Rumination in migraine: Mediating effects of brooding and reflection between migraine and psychological distress. *Psychology & Health*, 31:12,1481- 1497, DOI: 10.1080/08870446.2016.1235166

47.Lavoie K.L., Cartier A., Labrecque M., Bacon S.L., Lemière C., Malo J.L., Ditto B. (2005). Are psychiatric disorders associated with worse asthma control and quality of life in asthma patients?*RespiratoryMedicine*, 99, 10, 1249-1257.

48.Leplege, A, Ecosse, E, Verdier, A, Perneger, T.V. (1998). The French SF-36 Health survey: Translation, cultural adaptation and preliminary psychometric evaluation.J Clin Epidemiol5110131023

49.Linden W., Vodermaier A., Mackenzie R., Greig D. (2012). Anxiety and depression after cancer diagnosis: Prevalence rates by cancer type, gender, and age, *Journal of Affective Disorders.*

50.Linehan, M.M. (1993). Traitement cognitivo-comportemental du trouble de personnalité état limite, Bourg-Chêne: Médecine & Hygiène.

51. Matarazzo J. D., (1980), In Ogden J., (2014). *Psychology of health,* 2nd Ed. de Boeck.

52. Mikolajczak, M. (2013). *Interventions in health psychology.* Paris: Dunod.

53.Miller, W. R., & Rollnick, S. (2013). *Motivational interviewing - 2nd ed: Helping people to initiate change.* Paris: InterEditions.

54.Ministry of Health (2011). *What is a chronic disease?* Retrieved from the Necker website: http://www.maladiesrares-necker.aphp.fr/quest-quune-maladie-chronique/

55.Moullec, G., Lavoie, K. & Sultan, S. (2012). II. Affective vulnerability and health. *In Psychologie de la santé* (pp. 111-130). Paris: Presses Universitaires de France. doi:10.3917/puf.sulta.2012.01.0111.

56.Moskowitz, J. T., Carrico, A. W., Duncan, L. G., Cohn, M. A., Cheung, E. O., Batchelder, A. & Folkman, S. (2017). Randomized controlled trial of a positive affect intervention for people with newly diagnosed HIV. *Journal of Consulting and Clinical Psychology.*

57.Nolen-Hoeksema, S. (2004). The Response Styles Theory. In C. Papageorgiou, & A. Wells, (Eds), *Depressive rumination. Nature, theory and treatment* (pp. 107 - 123). Chichester: Wiley.

58.Nolen-Hoeksema S., Morrow J. (1993). "The Effects of Rumination and Distraction on Naturally-Occurring Depressed Moods", In Callahan, S. & Chabrol, H. (2013). *Mechanismes de défense etcoping.* Paris: Dunod.

59.Nolen-Hoeksema, S. (2000). The role of rumination in depressive disorders and mixed anxiety/depressive symptoms. *Journal of Abnormal Psychology*, 109, 504-511.

60.Nolen-Hoeksema, S., Wisco, B. E., & Lyubomirsky, S. (2008). Rethinking rumination. *Perspectives on Psychological Science,* 3, 400-424.

61.Ogden J., (2014). Chapter 9: Representations of illness. *Psychology of health*, 2nd Ed. de Boeck.

62. Philippot, P. (2011). Emotion and psychotherapy. Wavre, Belgium: Mardaga.

63. Philippot, P. & Douilliez, C. (2014). Emotion, cognition and behaviour: contribution of emotional models

to the understanding of anxiety. In *Les troubles anxieux* (pp. 6-17). Cachan: Lavoisier.

64. 2007-2011 national plan. *Pour l'amélioration de la qualité de vie des personnes atteintes de maladies chroniques* (2007). Ministry of Solidarity and Health.gouv

65. Pujol J.L., Launay M. & Boulze I., (2012). In Fernandez L., & Gaucher J., (2012). *Psychologie clinique de la santé : 12 études de cas.* Paris : In Press.

66. Raes F, Williams MG. The relationship between mindfulness and uncontrollability of ruminative thinking. *Mindfulness* 2010 in press.

67. Ribes G., (2012). Chapter 4 - Breast cancer, body image and sexuality. In Fernandez L., & Gaucher J., (2012). *Psychologie clinique de la santé : 12 études de cas.* Paris: InPress.

68. Ricci, A., Bonini, S., Cointinanza, M., Turano, M.T., Puliti, E.M., Finocchietti, A., Bertolucci, D. (2016). Worry and anger rumination in fibromyalgia syndrome. *Reumatismo*, 68(4):195-198

69. Roth B, Robbins D. Mindfulness-based stress reduction and health-related quality of life: findings from abilingual inner-city patient population. *PsychosomMed.* 2004; 66: 113-123

70. Schirda, B., Nicholas, J. A., & Prakash, R. S. (2015). Examining trait mindfulness, emotion dysregulation, and quality of life in multiple sclerosis. *Health Psychology*, *34*(11), 1107-1115.

71. Segal, Z. V., Williams, J. M. G., Teasdale, J. D. (2002). *Mindfulness-based cognitive therapy for depression: a new approach to preventing relapse.* New York: Guilford Press.

72. Segal, Z., Williams, J. M., & Teasdale, J. D. (2006). *Mindfulness-based cognitive therapy for depression: A new approach to relapse prevention,* Brussels: De Boek.

73. Seligman, M. E. P. (1994). *Learning Optimism.* Paris, InterEditions.

74. Seligman, M. E. P., Steen T. A., Park N. & Peterson C. (2005). Positive psychology Progress: empirical validation of interventions. *American psychologist*, vol 60 (5), 410-421.

75. Seligman, M.E.P., Rashid T. & Park A.C. (2006). Positive psychotherapy. *American Psychologist*, Vol 61(8), 774-788.

76. Seligman, M. E. P. & Csikszentmihalyi, M. (2011). Positive psychology: an introduction. In Martin-Krumm, C. & Tarquinio, C. (2011). *A treatise on positive psychology.* Brussels, DeBoeck.

77. Shankland, R. (2014). Chapter 11. The psychology of gratitude. In *Introduction to positive psychology* (pp. 167-179). Paris: Dunod. doi:10.3917/dunod.lecom.2014.01.0167.

78. Shankland, R., André, C., & Kotsou, I. (2015, June 01). Mindfulness and empathic responding.. Interuniversity Psychology Laboratory: http://www.lip.univ-savoie.fr/uploads/PDF/1845.pdf

79. Shapiro, S.L., Astin, J.A., Bishop, S.R., & Cordova, M. (2005). Mindfulness-based stress reductionfor health care professionals: Results from a randomized trial. *International Journal of Stress Management,* 12, 164-176

80. Sharma A., Kudesia P., Shi Q. & Gandhi, R. (2016). Anxiety and depression in patients with osteoarthritis: impact and management challenges. *Open Access Rheumatol.* 8:103- 13.doi:10.2147/OARRR.S93516

81. Skovlund, S. E. (2004). Diabetes attitudes, wishes and needs. *Diabetes Voice*, 49, 4-11.

82. Stober, J., & Borkovec, T. D. (2002). Reduced concreteness of worry in generalized anxiety disorder: Findings from a therapy study. *Cognitive Therapy and Research, 26*, 89-96.

83. Tang, N., Salkvskis, P., Hodges, A., Soong, E., Hanna, M. & Hester, J. 2009). Chronic pain syndrome associated with health anxiety: A qualitative thematic comparison between pain patients with high and low health anxiety. *British Journal ofClinical Psychology*, 48, 1-20

84. Teasdale, J. D. (2004). Mindfulness and the Third Wave of cognitive-behavioural therapies. In Kotsou, I. & Heeren, A. (2011). *Mindfulness and acceptance: Third wave therapies.* Louvain- la-Neuve, Belgium: De Boeck Supérieur.

85. Tignol, J. (2014). 18. Hypochondria or health anxiety. In *Les troubles anxieux* (pp. 191-201). Cachan: Lavoisier.

86. Thombs, B.D., Boss, E.B., Ford, D.E., Stewart, K.J., Tsilidis, K.K., Pateh, U., Fauerbacti, J.A., Bush, D.E. & Ziegelstei, R.C. (2006). Prevalence of depression in survivors of acute myocardial infarction: Review of the evidence. *Journal of General Internai Medicine* 21, 30-38.

87. Thompson, D.R. & Lewin, R.J.P. (2000). *Management of the post-myocardial infarction patient: rehabilitation and cardiac neurosis.* Heart, 84, 101-105.

88. Van Gordon, W., Shonin, E., Dunn, T. J., Garcia-Campayo, J., & Griffiths, M. D. (2017). Meditation awareness training for the treatment of fibromyalgia syndrome: A randomized controlled trial. *British Journal Of Health Psychology*, *22*(1), 186-206.

89. Van Son, J., Nyklicek, I., Nefs, G., Speight, J., Pop, V. J., & Pouwer, F. (2015). The associationbetween mindfulness and emotional distress in adults with diabetes: Could mindfulness serve as a buffer? Results from Diabetes MILES: The Netherlands. *Journal Of BehavioralMedicine*, *38*(2), 251-260.

90. Ware JE Jr, Sherbourne CD. The MOS 36-item short-form health survey (SF-36). I. Conceptual framework and item selection. Med Care. 1992;30:473-483

91. Watkins, E., & Brown, R. G. (2002). Rumination and executive function in depression: an experimental study. *Journal of Neurology, Neurosurgery, and Psychiatry*, 72, 400-402.

92. Watkins, E., & Moulds, M. (2005). Distinct modes of ruminative self-focus: Impact of abstract versus concrete rumination on problem solving in depression. *Emotion*, *5*(3), 319-328.

93. Watkins, E. R. (2008). Constructive and unconstructive repetitive thought. *Psychological Bulletin*, 134, 163-206.

94. Watkins, 2008 In Philippot, P. (2011). *Emotion and psychotherapy.* Wavre, Belgium: Mardaga.

95. Watkins, E. R., Baeyens, C. S., Read, R. (2009). Concreteness training reduces dysphoria: proof-of-principle for repeated cognitive bias modification in depression. *Journal Abnormal Psychology*, 118, 5564.

96. Watkins, E.R., Moberly, N.J. (2009). Concreteness training reduces dysphoria: a pilot proof-of-principle study. *Behaviour Research and Therapy*, 47, 48-53.

97. Zigmond A.S., SnaithR.P. The Hospital Anxiety and Depression Scale. Acta Psychiatr. Scand. 1983, 67, 361-370. French translation: J.F. Lépine, 1985

Appendix 1: Classification of the 6 virtues and 24 strengths by Seligman and Peterson (2005)

Virtues	Associated forces
Wisdom and Knowledge	• Creativity

	• Curiosity
	• Open-mindedness
	• Love of learning
	• Wisdom
Courage	- Bravery
	- Perseverance
	- Authenticity
	- Vitality
Humanity	• Love
	• Kindness
	• Social intelligence
... **Justice**	• Group work
	• Sense of fairness
	• Leadership
Temperance	• Sorry
	• Modesty
	• Caution
	• Self-control
Transcendence	• Appreciation of beauty and excellence
	• Gratitude
	• Optimism
	• Humour
	• Spirituality

Appendix 2: Detailed view of the MBI programme (A, Fontaine & M, Laval)

Sessions	Content
Session 1	• Home presentation
	• Grape exercise
	• Body scan
	• film Sarah Lazar
Session 2	• Body scan
	• Wanderlust and a tendency to judge
	• First anchor breath + posture
	• Sitting meditation 15-20' (breathing presence here and now)
Session 3	• 3'ER
	• Standing yoga
	• Sitting meditation 20' (breath and safe place)
Session 4	• 4 elements

	• Meditation walk
	• Sitting meditation 30' (Emotional climate)
Session 5	• 3'ER
	• Yoga on the floor
	• Exploring difficult situations
	• Sitting meditation
	• ACT matrix
	• meditation pleasant situation
Session 6	• Sitting meditation sounds
	• Work in relation to our judgements, thoughts
	• Identification of cognitive distortions
	• Sitting meditation
Session 7	• Meditation to music
	• Mountain Meditation
	• Adjustment strategies
	• Meditation without purpose
Session 8	• Minutes
	• Sitting meditations

Appendix 3: Detailed view of the CARE programme (Shankland. André. Kotosu. 2015)

Sessions	Content
Session 1	• Group dynamics • Satisfying events to relive • My strengths • Satisfying events diary
Session 2	• A project that gave me satisfaction • My strengths in action • Strengths in others • Using your strengths
Session 3	• My strengths in the face of a problem • Being present in the moment • Environmental forces
Session 4	• Activities that do you good • Commitment to actions in line with my values • Focus on events that are satisfying for others • Being kind to yourself
Session 5	• Being my best friend • Rediscovering a loved one/ paying attention to others • Taking care of what is meaningful to you • A step towards a project in line with your values
Session 6	• Activity that does me good

	• Gratitude journal	
Session 7	• Letter of gratitude • Exploring other points of view • Obstacles are experiences • Taking care of the environment • Caring for others/the environment • Satisfactory interactions	
Session 8	• Appreciating the present moment • Programme review • Continuing practices after CARE	

Appendix 4: Scatter plots (boxplot)

Scatterplots of the CARE group in the two dimensions of SF-36 at Tl and T2

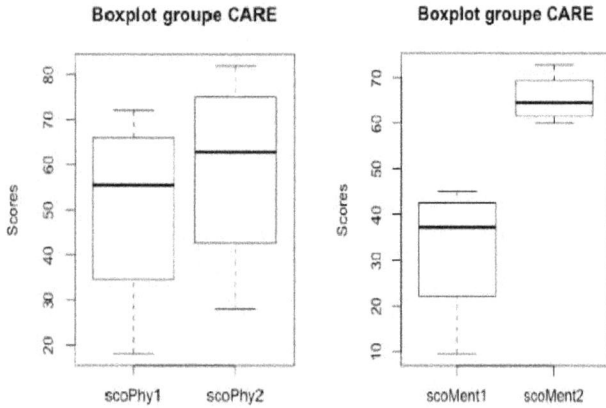

Boxplot groupe CARE — Boxplot groupe CARE

Scatterplots of the CARE group in the two HADS dimensions at T1 and T2

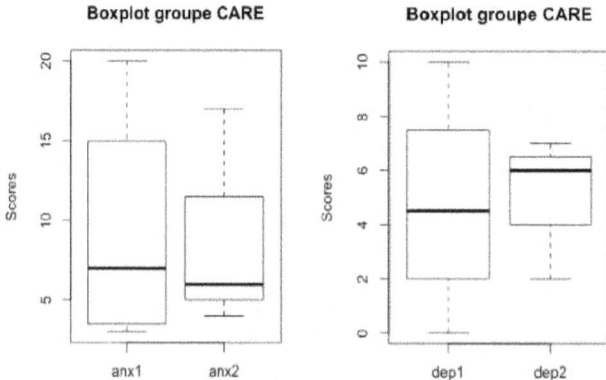

Boxplot groupe CARE — Boxplot groupe CARE

34

Scatterplots of the CARE group in the two dimensions of the mini-Certs at T1 and T2

Boxplot groupe CARE

Boxplot groupe CARE

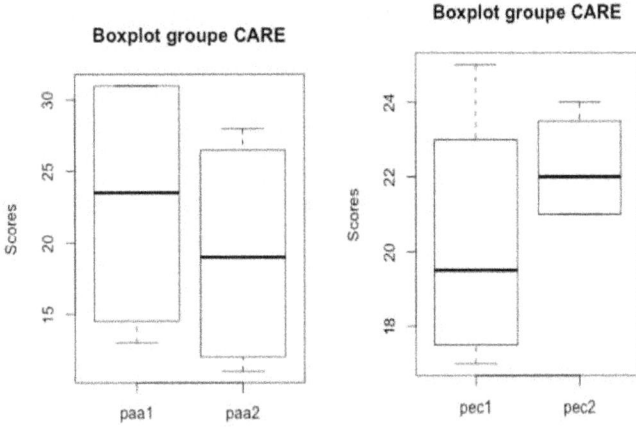

Scatterplots of the MBI group in the two dimensions of the SF-36 at T1 and T2

Boxplot groupe MBI

Boxplot groupe MBI

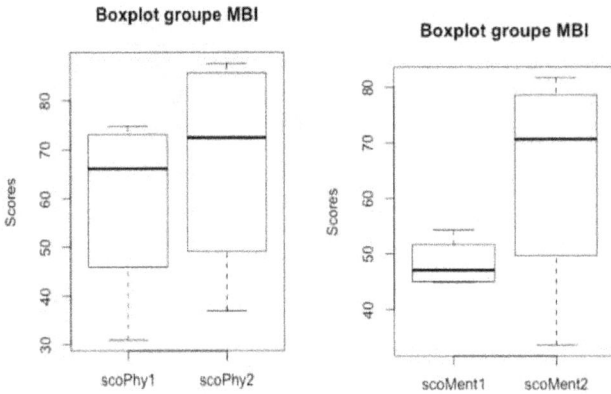

Scatterplots of the MBI group in the two HADS dimensions at T1 and T2

Boxplot groupe MBI

Boxplot groupe MBI

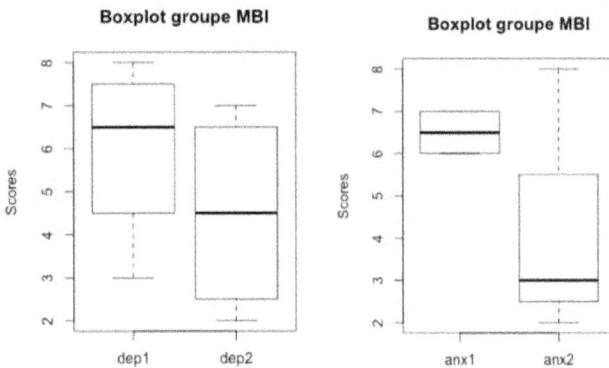

Scatterplots of the MBI group in the two dimensions of the mini-CERTS at Tl and T2

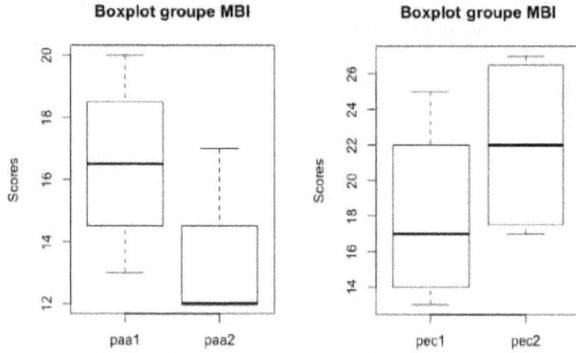

Boxplot groupe MBI

Boxplot groupe MBI

Appendix 5: Average scores obtained by the CARE group on the SF-35 sub-dimensions at T1 and T2

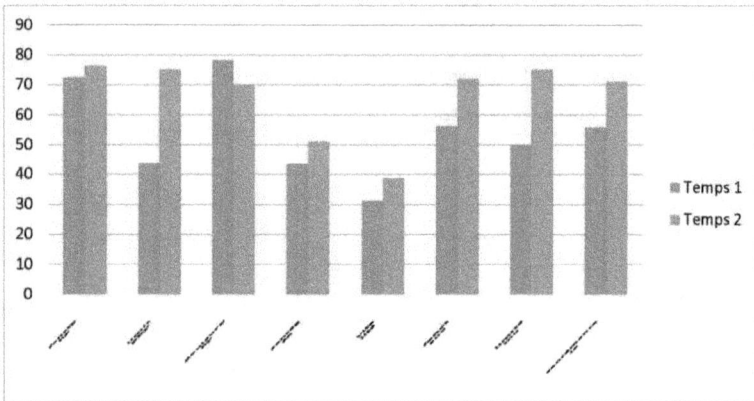

Appendix 6: Average scores obtained by the MBI group on the SF-35 sub-dimensions at T1 and T2

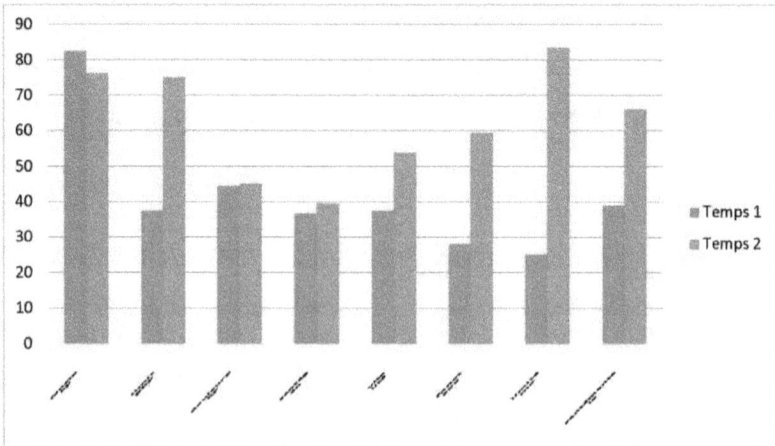

Summary table of data obtained from the SF-36, HADS and Mini-Certs questionnaires by each participant at T1 and T2

Group	scophysl	scophys2	scomentl	scoment2	anxl	anx2	depl	dep2	paal	paa2	ped	pec2
care	18,12	28	9,5	60	4	6	4	7	31	28	18	23
care	72	82	34,75	72,8	20	17	5	6	31	25	25	21
care	51	57,3	40	66	10	4	10	6	13	11	17	21
care	60	68,3	45	63	3	6	0	2	16	13	21	24
mbi	74,8	37	45,1	33,5	7	8	3	7	20	17	15	18
mbi	31	61,25	44,9	65,87	7	3	7	3	17	12	25	26
mbi	71,4	83,75	49	81,75	6	2	8	2	16	12	19	Tl
mbi	60,83	87,7	54,3	75,5	6	3	6	6	13	12	13	17

SF-36

Instructions - How to answer :

The following questions are about your health, as you feel it. This information will give us a better idea of how you feel in your everyday life. Please answer all the questions by circling the number corresponding to your chosen answer, as indicated. If you're not sure how to answer, choose the answer closest to your situation

1 - **Overall, do you think your health is :**

circle the answer of your choice

- excellent   1
- very good   2
- good   3
- mediocre   4
- bad   5

2 - **Compared to this time last year, how do you feel about your health at the moment?**

circle the answer of your choice

- much better than last year   1
- rather better   2
- about the same   3
- rather less good   4
- much less good 5 **3 - Here is a list of activities you may have to do in your daily life. For each one, indicate whether your current state of health makes it difficult for you.**

circle the answer of your choice one per line

Activity list	Yes, very embarrassed	Yes, a little embarras	No, not at all embarrass

		sed	ed
3a - heavy physical exertion such as running, heavy lifting, sport	1	2	3
3b - moderate physical exertion such as moving a table, vacuuming, bowls	1	2	3
3c - lifting and carrying groceries	1	2	3
3d - climbing several flights of stairs	1	2	3
3e - climbing a flight of stairs	1	2	3
3f - bending forward, kneeling, crouching	1	2	3
3g - walk more than 1 km	1	2	3
3h - walk several hundred metres	1	2	3
3i - walk a hundred metres	1	2	3
3j - bathing, showering or dressing	1	2	3

4 - Over the last 4 weeks, and because of your physical condition

circle the answer of your choice one per line

	YES	NO
4a - Have you reduced the amount of time you spend at work or on your usual activities?	1	2
4b - did you do less than you would have liked?	1	2
4c - have you had to stop doing certain things?	1	2
4d - did you have any difficulties doing your work or any other activity?	1	2

5 - Over the last 4 weeks, and because of your emotional state (feeling sad, nervous or depressed)

circle the answer of your choice one per line

	YES	NO
5a - Have you reduced the amount of time you spend at work or on your usual activities?	1	2
5b - did you do less than you would have liked?	1	2
5c - did you find it difficult to do what you had to do with the same care and attention?	1	2

6 - Over the last 4 weeks, to what extent has your physical or emotional state of health hindered you in your life and in your relationships with others, your family, friends and acquaintances?

circle the answer of your choice

- not at all   1

- a little bit   2
- medium   3
- many   4
- very much   5

7 - Over the last 4 weeks, how much (physical) pain have you experienced?

circle the answer of your choice

- nil   1
- very low   2
- low   3
- average   4
- big   5
- very large   6

8 - Over the last four weeks, has your pain interfered with your work or domestic activities?

circle the answer of your choice

- not at all   1
- a little bit   2
- moderately   3
- a lot   4
- a lot   5

9 - The following questions ask how you have been feeling over the last 4 weeks.

For each question, please indicate the answer that seems most appropriate to you

In the last 4 weeks, have there been times when :

circle the answer of your choice one per line

	at permanence	very often	often	sometimes	rarely	never
9a - did you feel dynamic?	1	2	3	4	5	6
9b - did you feel very nervous?	1	2	3	4	5	6
9c - you felt so discouraged that nothing could cheer you up?	1	2	3	4	5	6
9d - did you feel calm and relaxed?	1	2	3	4	5	6
9th - did you feel full of energy?	1	2	3	4	5	6
9f - did you feel sad or down?	1	2	3	4	5	6
9g - did you feel exhausted?	1	2	3	4	5	6
9am - did you feel good about yourself?	1	2	3	4	5	6
9i - did you feel tired?	1	2	3	4	5	6

39

10 - In the last 4 weeks, have there been times when your state of health, either physical or emotional, has interfered with your life or your relationships with others, your family, friends or acquaintances?

circle the answer of your choice

- all the time   1
- a good part of the time   2
  - from time to time   3
  - rarely   4
  - j amais   5

11 - For each of the following sentences, indicate to what extent they are true or false in your case:

circle the answer of your choice one per line

	Totally true	Quite true	I don't know	Rather false	Totally false
lia - I fall ill more easily than others	1	2	3	4	5
llb - I'm as healthy as anyone else	1	2	3	4	5
llc - I expect my health to deteriorate	1	2	3	4	5
llc - I'm in good health	1	2	3	4	5

Please check that you have provided an answer for each question.

Tool associated with the good practice recommendation "Stopping smoking: from individual screening to maintaining abstinence".

maintaining abstinence".

HAD scale: *Hospital Anxiety and Depression scale*

The HAD scale is an instrument used to screen for anxiety and depressive disorders. It comprises 14 items rated from 0 to 3. Seven questions relate to anxiety (total A) and seven to depression (total D), giving two scores (maximum score for each = 21).

1. I feel tense or irritated
- Most of the time3
- Often2
- From time to time1
- Never0

2. I enjoy the same things I used to
- Yes, just as much0
- Not as much1
- Only a little2
- Almost no more3

3. I have a feeling of fear as if something horrible is going to happen to me

- Yes, very clearly3
- Yes, but it's not too serious 2
- A little, but that doesn't worry me 1
- Not at all0

4. **I laugh easily and look on the bright side of things**
- As much as in the past0
- Not as much as before1
- Much less than before2
- Not at all3

5. **I'm worried**
- Very often3
- Quite often2
- Occasionally1
- Very occasionally 0

6. **I'm in a good mood**
- Never3
- Rarely2
- Quite often1
- Most of the time0

7. **I can sit quietly doing nothing and feel relaxed.**
- Yes, whatever happens0
- Yes, in general1
- Rarely2
- Never3

8. **I feel like I'm running in slow motion**
- Almost always3
- Very often2
- Sometimes1
- Never0

9. **I have feelings of fear and a knot in my stomach**
- Never0
- Sometimes1
- Quite often2
- Very often3

10. **I'm no longer interested in my appearance**
- Not at all3
- I don't pay as much attention to it as I should2
- I may not pay as much attention to it any more
1I pay as much attention to it as I did in the past 0

11. **I'm restless and can't keep still**
- Yes, that's exactly the case3
- A little2

41

- Not so much1
- Not at all0

12. I'm looking forward to doing certain things
- As much as before0
- Slightly less than before1
- Much less than before2
- Almost never3

13. I have sudden feelings of panic
- Very, very often3
- Quite often2
- Not very often1
- Never0

14. I can enjoy a good book or a good radio or television programme.
- Often0
- Sometimes1
- Rarely2
- Very rarely3

Tool associated with the good practice recommendation "Stopping smoking: from individual screening

to maintaining abstinence".

Scores

Add up the points for the following answers: 1, 3, 5, 7, 9, 11, 13: Total A = 2

Add up the points for the following answers: 2, 4, 6, 8,10,12, 14: Total D = 1.

Interpretation

To screen for anxiety and depressive symptoms, the following interpretation can be proposed for each of the scores (A and D):

- 7 or less: no symptoms
- 8 to 10: doubtful symptoms - 11 and over: definite symptoms.

Depending on the results, it may be necessary to seek specialist advice.

References

- Zigmond A.S., Snaith R.P. *The Hospital Anxiety andDepression Scale. Acta Psychiatr. Scand*, 1983, 67, 361-370. French translation: J.F. Lépine.
  - "L'évaluation clinique standardisée en psychiatrie", edited by J.D. Guelfi, published by Pierre Fabre. Also presented in: Pratiques médicales et thérapeutiques, April 2000, 2, 31.

Read each of the suggestions below, then mark with a cross the box that best describes what you usually experience. Don't spend too much time answering, it's your first impression that's important.

"When thoughts about myself, my feelings or situations and events that I have experienced come to mind...".

	Almost	Sometimes	Often	Almost

	never			always
1. My thoughts are stuck in a rut, always returning to the same themes				
2. I can understand and respond to changes intuitively, without having to analyse everything in detail				
3. I compare myself to other people				
4. I think about it openly, freely and creatively				
5. I judge myself according to my personal values and beliefs				
6. I focus on the question of why things happened the way they did				
7. I wonder why I can't get into action				
8. My thoughts develop in new and interesting directions				
9. I seem to be immersed in the action and in touch with what's going on around me				
10. I don't think I'm good at anything				
11. I like to let myself go with the flow of my spontaneous thoughts				
12. I feel under pressure to prevent my worst fears coming true				
13. I concentrate on exploring and playing with ideas, curious about where they might lead me.				
14. My thoughts tend to flow from a specific event to broader, more general aspects of my life.				
15. I don't care what other people think of me				
16. I quickly get impressions and intuitions about what's going on and how to react				

Douilliez et al (20012) ©.

Quotation

The items were rated on a scale from *1 (almost never)* to *4 (almost always)*.

43

PPA: items 1, 3, 6, 7, 10, 12, 14, 15
PEC: items 2, 4, 8, 9, 11, 13, 16
Douilliez et al (20012) ©.

www.ingramcontent.com/pod-product-compliance
Lightning Source LLC
Chambersburg PA
CBHW021824270326
41932CB00007B/329